姉妹都市を周遊しながら四技能を身につけよう

Twin Cities
A Cross-cultural Connection

Bradley G. Smith
Neil T. Millington
Anna Millington

Twin Cities—A Cross-cultural Connection

Bradley G. Smith / Neil T. Millington / Anna Millington

© 2017 Cengage Learning K.K.

ALL RIGHTS RESERVED. No part of this work covered by the copyright herein may be reproduced, transmitted, stored, or used in any form or by any means—graphic, electronic, or mechanical, including but not limited to photocopying, recording, scanning, digitizing, taping, Web distribution, information networks, or information storage and retrieval systems—without the prior written permission of the publisher.

Photo Credits:
Cover: © (T) The Asahi Shimbun/Getty Images, (B) © Robertus Pudyanto/Getty Images News/Getty Images;
p. 9: © The Asahi Shimbun/Getty Images; p. 10: © Ablestock.com/Thinkstock;
p. 13: © Archives21/Pacific Press Service; p. 14: © Archives21/Pacific Press Service;
p. 17: © Archives21/Pacific Press Service; p. 18: © Grigory Fedyukovich/iStock/Thinkstock;
p. 21: © UniversalImagesGroup/Getty Images; p. 22: © EPA=Jiji;
p. 25: © javarman3/iStock/Thinkstock; p. 26: © dpa=Jiji Press Photo;
p. 29: © HIT1912/iStock/Thinkstock; p. 30: © TheYok/iStock/Thinkstock;
p. 33: © Peera_Sathawirawong/iStock/Thinkstock; p. 34: © Alamy/Pacific Press Service;
p. 37: © MIXA/Getty Images News/Getty Images; p. 38: © Alamy/Pacific Press Service;
p. 41: © DEA/W. BUSS/De Agostini/Getty Images; p. 42: © Dmytro Kosmenko/iStock/Thinkstock;
p. 45: © Bloomberg/Getty Images; p. 46: © Alamy/Pacific Press Service;
p. 49: © vichie81/iStock/Thinkstock; p. 50: © Thinkstock/Stockbyte/Thinkstock;
p. 53: © kuppa_rock/iStock/Thinkstock; p. 54: © yuruphoto/iStock/Thinkstock;
p. 57: © The Asahi Shimbun/Getty Images; p. 58: © Robertus Pudyanto/Getty Images News/Getty Images;
p. 61: © Jiji Press Photo; p. 62: © Pascal Le Segretain/Getty Images News/Getty Images;
p. 65: © The Asahi Shimbun/Getty Images; p. 66: © Brandon Seidel/iStock/Thinkstock

For permission to use material from this textbook or product, e-mail to elt@cengagejapan.com

ISBN: 978-4-86312-310-6

Cengage Learning K.K.
No. 2 Funato Building 5th Floor
1-11-11 Kudankita, Chiyoda-ku
Tokyo 102-0073
Japan

Tel: 03-3511-4392
Fax: 03-3511-4391

Preface

Twin cities are two cities that share a special cultural and economic relationship. They bond together by sharing with each other. They might exchange art, technology, and education. As a member of the global community, Japan's cities have made these important links by creating and maintaining twin city relationships with cities around the world. These twin cities relationships can serve as a way for Japanese people to gain a deeper understanding of foreign cultures.

This textbook will take you on an exciting journey around the world in order to explore Japan's connections to foreign people through its twin cities relationships. The content of each unit is designed around a Japanese city's relationship with one of its twin cities. The activities will help you to strengthen your English abilities in the four skills: reading, writing, speaking, and listening. We are confident that this textbook will help you to improve your English and gain a better understanding of foreign cultures.

Bradley G. Smith, Neil T. Millington, and Anna Millington

....

はしがき

本書『Twin Cities』は、リーディング、ライティング、スピーキング、リスニングの4つのスキルアップを目的とした総合英語テキストです。姉妹都市である日本と外国の都市間での文化交流やつながりについて学ぶことによって、外国の文化をより深く理解することができます。それに加えて、日本の都市についても知ることができ、これらの都市が共通点を持つ世界の都市と、どのように姉妹都市の関係を築き上げてきたのか理解することができます。本書での学習を通して、学生の皆さんが国際関係や世界の文化への関心を高め、その理解を深めるきっかけとなれば幸いです。

著者一同

Contents

Preface（はしがき） ……………………… 3
本書の構成と効果的な使い方 ……… 6
Glossary ………………………………… 69

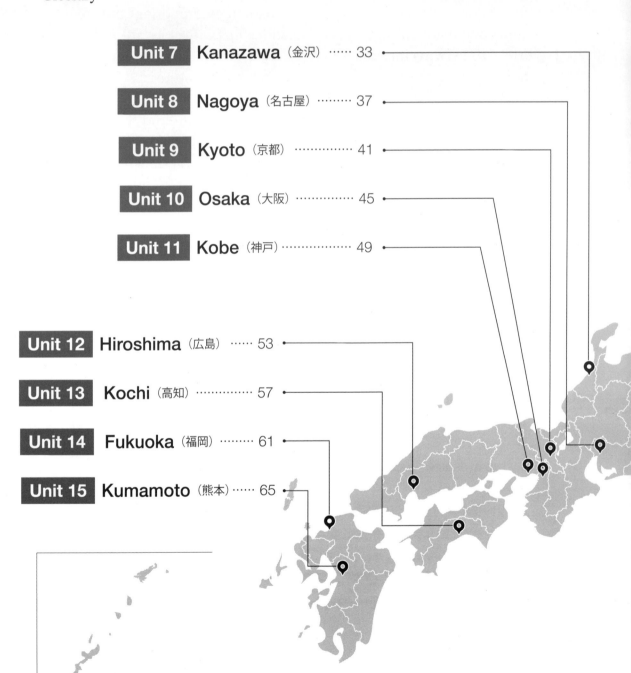

| Unit 7 | Kanazawa（金沢）…… 33
| Unit 8 | Nagoya（名古屋）…… 37
| Unit 9 | Kyoto（京都）………… 41
| Unit 10 | Osaka（大阪）………… 45
| Unit 11 | Kobe（神戸）………… 49
| Unit 12 | Hiroshima（広島）…… 53
| Unit 13 | Kochi（高知）………… 57
| Unit 14 | Fukuoka（福岡）……… 61
| Unit 15 | Kumamoto（熊本）…… 65

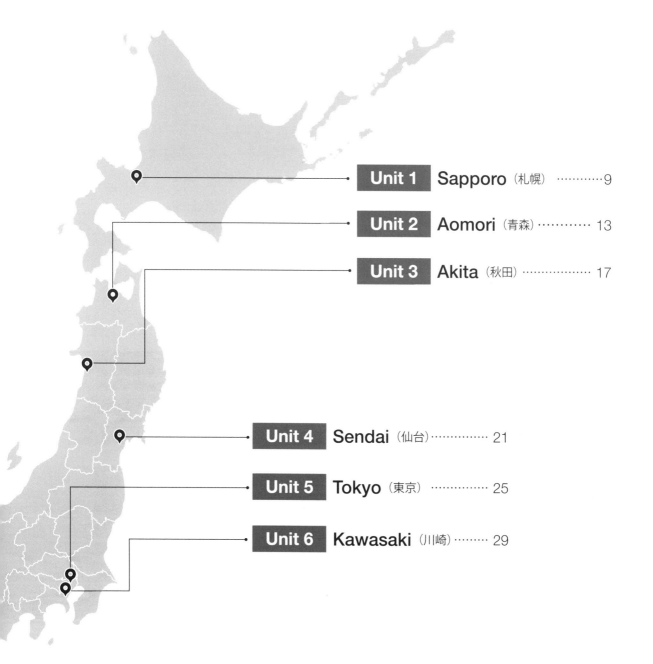

Unit 1　Sapporo（札幌）……… 9
Unit 2　Aomori（青森）……… 13
Unit 3　Akita（秋田）……… 17
Unit 4　Sendai（仙台）……… 21
Unit 5　Tokyo（東京）……… 25
Unit 6　Kawasaki（川崎）……… 29

本書の構成と効果的な使い方

本書は全部で15ユニットから構成され、ユニットごとに1つの日本の都市とその海外の姉妹都市を取り上げています。また、巻末には各ユニットの重要語句を一覧にしたGlossaryを収録しています。

[各ユニットの基本構成とアクティビティの特徴]

1ページ目

 Guessing Twin Cities

提示されている6つの都市がユニットで取り上げる日本の都市と姉妹都市であるかどうかを答えるクイズ形式のウオーミングアップです。先生からヒントを英語で聞き、どれが姉妹都市かを推測しましょう。

 Building-up Vocabulary

本文から厳選した、基本的かつ重要な8つの語句の日本語の意味をインプットし、リーディングの他、あとに続くリスニング、スピーキング、ライティングのアクティビティに役立てたり使ったりしながら、運用できる語彙力を身につけ、英語力アップの基礎を固めましょう。

2ページ目

Reading Practice

200語程度の本文のリーディングです。海外の姉妹都市1つを取り上げ、前半はその都市の紹介、後半は日本の都市との関係について述べています。本文の下の語注も参照しながら、内容の理解に努めましょう。

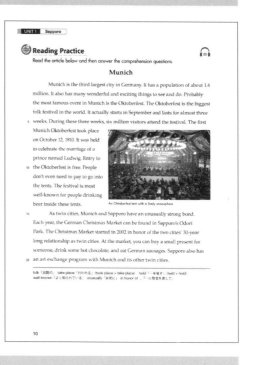

3ページ目

Comprehension Questions

T/F形式の問題でReading Practiceで読んだ本文内容の理解度をチェックします。ペアになって、順番に英語の問題文を読み合いながら解答すれば、リスニングとスピーキングの練習にもなります。

Brainstorming

次のアクティビティのためのウオーミングアップです。日本の都市に関して自分が知っていることをグループで話し合い、それをクラスに英語でシェアします。

Listening Practice

リスニングによる英文完成問題です。日本の都市（やその都市が属する都道府県）に関する情報や特徴などについて書かれた英文を音声で聴き、空所を埋めましょう。

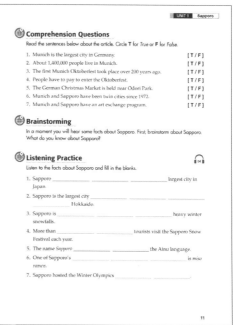

4ページ目

 **Working in a Group**

Reading Practice の本文や Listening Practice の英文で言及された内容をトピックとして提示しています。グループ内の数名で質問に答えながら自分たちの意見をまとめ、グループ全体でお互いに意見交換をしましょう。このアクティビティを通して、協力して取り組む力やコミュニケーション力、思考力の養成も図ります。

 **Writing Practice**

最後にユニットで学んだ知識をライティングで表現します。Reading Practice の本文や Listening Practice の英文で言及された内容をトピックとして提示し、それに関する自分の経験や考えを書きましょう。

音声ファイルの無料ダウンロード

http://cengage.jp/elt/JapaneseFourSkills/

 のアイコンがある箇所の音声ファイルをダウンロードできます。

❶ 上記 URL にアクセスまたは QR コードをスマートフォンなどのリーダーでスキャン（→❹へ）
❷ 本書の表紙画像またはタイトル（Twin Cities）をクリック
❸ 本書のページで 音声ファイル ボタンをクリック
❹ 希望の番号をクリックして音声ファイルをダウンロード

UNIT 1

Sapporo

🌐 Guessing Twin Cities

Two of these cities are twinned with Sapporo. Can you guess which ones?

Cities	Yes or No	Cities	Yes or No
Manila, The Philippines		Paris, France	
Moscow, Russia		Portland, Oregon, USA	
Munich, Germany		Stockholm, Sweden	

🌐 Building-up Vocabulary

 02

Match the words with the Japanese meanings from the box below.

English	Japanese	English	Japanese
population		marriage	
million		entry	
last		bond	
celebrate		relationship	

人口	参加	関係	きずな
結婚	100万の	続く	…を祝う

Munich

Munich is the third largest city in Germany. It has a population of about 1.4 million. It also has many wonderful and exciting things to see and do. Probably the most famous event in Munich is the Oktoberfest. The Oktoberfest is the biggest folk festival in the world. It actually starts in September and lasts for almost three weeks. During these three weeks, six million visitors attend the festival. The first Munich Oktoberfest took place on October 12, 1810. It was held to celebrate the marriage of a prince named Ludwig. Entry to the Oktoberfest is free. People don't even need to pay to go into the tents. The festival is most well-known for people drinking beer inside these tents.

An Oktoberfest tent with a lively atmosphere

As twin cities, Munich and Sapporo have an unusually strong bond. Each year, the German Christmas Market can be found in Sapporo's Odori Park. The Christmas Market started in 2002 in honor of the two cities' 30-year long relationship as twin cities. At the market, you can buy a small present for someone, drink some hot chocolate, and eat German sausages. Sapporo also has an art exchange program with Munich and its other twin cities.

---

folk「民間の」 take place「行われる」(took place > take place) hold「…を催す」(held > hold)
well-known「よく知られている」 unusually「非常に」 in honor of ...「…に敬意を表して」

Comprehension Questions

Read the sentences below about the article. Circle **T** for *True* or **F** for *False*.

1. Munich is the largest city in Germany.   [T / F]
2. About 1,400,000 people live in Munich.   [T / F]
3. The first Munich Oktoberfest took place over 200 years ago.   [T / F]
4. People have to pay to enter the Oktoberfest.   [T / F]
5. The German Christmas Market began less than 10 years ago.   [T / F]
6. Munich and Sapporo have been twin cities since 1972.   [T / F]
7. Munich and Sapporo have an art exchange program.   [T / F]

Brainstorming

In a moment you will hear some facts about Sapporo. First, brainstorm about Sapporo. What do you know about Sapporo?

Listening Practice

Listen to the facts about Sapporo and fill in the blanks.

1. Sapporo _____ _____ _____ largest city in Japan.
2. Sapporo is the largest city _____ _____ _____ _____ Hokkaido.
3. Sapporo is _____ _____ _____ heavy winter snowfalls.
4. More than _____ _____ tourists visit the Sapporo Snow Festival each year.
5. The name *Sapporo* _____ _____ the Ainu language.
6. One of Sapporo's _____ _____ _____ is *miso ramen*.
7. Sapporo hosted the Winter Olympics _____ _____.

UNIT 1 Sapporo

🌐 Working in a Group

Work with your group. Prepare some answers to these questions about a popular festival that you know about.

1. What is one of the most popular festivals?
   _____

2. When is it celebrated?
   _____

3. Do you enjoy going to this festival? Why or why not?
   _____

4. Are there any special foods connected with this festival?
   _____

5. What are some of the things that are usually done at this festival?
   _____

🌐 Writing Practice

Write about a holiday you have been on. Try to answer these questions.

1. Where did you go?
   _____

2. Who did you go with?
   _____

3. When did you go there?
   _____

4. What did you do there?
   _____

5. How did you get there?
   _____

6. Why did you go there?
   _____

UNIT 2

Aomori

Guessing Twin Cities

Two of these cities are twinned with Aomori City. Can you guess which ones?

Cities	Yes or No	Cities	Yes or No
Cape Town, South Africa		Helsinki, Finland	
Dalian, China		New Delhi, India	
Glasgow, Scotland		Pyeongtaek, South Korea	

Building-up Vocabulary

Match the words with the Japanese meanings from the box below.

English	Japanese	English	Japanese
major		similar	
port		information	
trade		attend	
bloom		influence	

（花が）咲く	（学校）に通う	似ている	港
情報	影響	貿易	主要な

13

UNIT 2　Aomori

Reading Practice

Read the article below and then answer the comprehension questions.

Dalian

Dalian is a major port city in northeastern China. More than six million people live there. Being one of the largest foreign trade ports in China, Dalian is a city with many international festivals and events. The Dalian (Lushun) International Cherry Blossom Festival is held each year in April and May. People come from around the world to see the many beautiful cherry blossoms bloom.

Dalian also hosts an International Beer Festival every July and August. Visitors can enjoy drinking beer from all around China and the world. It is similar to Oktoberfest in Munich, Germany. Dalian's International Fashion Festival takes place in September. Dalian is famous in China as a place for fashion.

Overlooking Dalian's large, busy port

Aomori City and Dalian became twin cities in late 2004. There is much cooperation between the two cities. Aomori has a strong business relationship with Dalian, especially in the information technology (IT) sector. Universities in Aomori have also created international partnerships with those in Dalian. Many students from Dalian have been part of exchange programs to attend schools in Aomori. Dalian's relationship with Aomori and the rest of Japan has had a very strong influence on both cities. You can see this yourself if you visit Dalian. There is a street called Japanese Street with many kinds of Japanese shops, restaurants, and tea houses.

---

cherry blossom「サクラの花」　cooperation「協力」　sector「部門」　partnership「提携」　rest「残り」
tea house「茶室」

UNIT 2   Aomori

Comprehension Questions

Read the sentences below about the article. Circle **T** for *True* or **F** for *False*.

1. Dalian is located in southwestern China. [T / F]
2. Dalian has many international festivals and events. [T / F]
3. The International Cherry Blossom Festival is held each year. [T / F]
4. The International Beer Festival happens in April. [T / F]
5. Aomori City and Dalian became twin cities in late 2014. [T / F]
6. Aomori has a strong business relationship with Dalian. [T / F]
7. There is a street called Japanese Street in Dalian. [T / F]

Brainstorming

In a moment you will hear some facts about Aomori City/Prefecture. First, brainstorm about Aomori. What do you know about Aomori?

Listening Practice

Listen to the facts about Aomori and fill in the blanks.

1. Aomori Prefecture is in _____ _____ _____ _____ the island of Honshu.
2. Aomori City has a population of about _____ _____.
3. The Hakkoda Mountains lie _____ _____ _____ _____ Aomori City.
4. Aomori Nebuta is a _____ festival that _____ _____ from August _____ _____ _____.
5. Hitoshi Saito _____ _____ judo player from Aomori _____ _____ _____ Olympic Gold medals.
6. Aomori Prefecture's _____ and seafood are _____ _____ Japan.
7. There are old houses _____ _____ _____ _____ _____ on Shinmachi Street.

15

UNIT 2   Aomori

Working in a Group

Work with your group. Prepare some answers to these questions about a famous person you know about.

1. What is his/her name?

2. Why is he/she famous?

3. What does he/she do?

4. What would you do if you could spend a day with this person?

5. Would you like to be famous like this person? Why or why not?

Writing Practice

Write about a place of natural beauty you have been to. Try to answer these questions.

1. Where is this place?

2. Who did you go there with?

3. When did you go there?

4. What can people do there?

5. How did you get there?

6. Why did you go there?

UNIT 3

Akita

🌐 Guessing Twin Cities

Three of these cities are twinned with Akita City. Can you guess which ones?

Cities	Yes or No	Cities	Yes or No
Ankara, Turkey		St. Cloud, Minnesota, USA	
Passau, Germany		Vancouver, Canada	
Rio de Janeiro, Brazil		Vladivostok, Russia	

🌐 Building-up Vocabulary

Match the words with the Japanese meanings from the box below.

English	Japanese	English	Japanese
pleasant		public	
predict		traditional	
recently		manufacturer	
host		citizen	

…を予測する	…を主催する	近ごろ	市民
（天気が）気持ちのよい	伝統的な	公開の	製造業者

Reading Practice

Read the article below and then answer the comprehension questions.

Vladivostok

Vladivostok is a port city in the far east of Russia. The city has a population of nearly 600,000 people. It is very cold in winter, but the summers can be quite pleasant and sunny. Overall, the weather is very hard to predict. It can be foggy, rainy, and sunny all in the same day! Vladivostok has many interesting things
5   to see and do. Recently, Vladivostok has become an attraction for musicians around the world. The city hosts an international jazz festival every November. There is also a famous music festival held in
10 the summer called V-ROX. Music fans come from everywhere to watch many kinds of music being played at the festival. It is like a huge summer party.

Vladivostok—a modern city under a cloudy sky

15   Akita City and Vladivostok have been twin cities since 1992. The cities have a sports and cultural exchange program. They have also held public performances of traditional dramas and dancing in each other's cities. Since Vladivostok imports almost 250,000 Japanese cars per year, Akita's car parts manufacturers have shown interest in developing a stronger trade relationship with the city. The student and
20 teacher exchange program between the two cities is a great way for citizens of both cities to learn about each other's culture. One example of this is that Russian students at Vladivostok's Far Eastern Federal University can study Japanese and even participate in a *haiku* contest.

---

overall「全体的に」 weather「天気」 sunny「晴れた」 since「…以来、…であるから」
interest in ...「…に対する興味」 participate in ...「…に参加する」

UNIT 3   Akita

Comprehension Questions

Read the sentences below about the article. Circle **T** for *True* or **F** for *False*.

1. Vladivostok has more than one million people.   [T / F]
2. Every day is sunny and warm in Vladivostok.   [T / F]
3. Vladivostok hosts a jazz festival every summer.   [T / F]
4. Akita City and Vladivostok have held public performances in each other's cities.   [T / F]
5. Vladivostok imports almost 150,000 Japanese cars every year.   [T / F]
6. There is a student exchange program between Vladivostok and Akita City.   [T / F]
7. Russian students can study Japanese at Far Eastern Federal University. [T / F]

Brainstorming

In a moment you will hear some facts about Akita City/Prefecture. First, brainstorm about Akita. What do you know about Akita?

Listening Practice

Listen to the facts about Akita and fill in the blanks.

1. Mount Taihei is _____ _____ _____ and it turns a beautiful rainbow _____ _____ in the fall.
2. Inaniwa *udon* _____ _____ _____ _____ of Akita Prefecture.
3. Senshu Park is a _____ _____ _____ _____ cherry blossoms.
4. Kanto Festival is _____ _____ attraction _____ _____ _____ in Akita Prefecture.
5. The Sea of Japan is only a _____-_____ _____ from the center of Akita City.
6. The *Akita no Gyoji* is one of _____ _____ paintings _____ _____ _____.
7. Akita City _____ _____ wonderful jazz and dance festivals _____ _____.

UNIT 3   Akita

Working in a Group

Work with your group. Prepare some answers to these questions about music.

1. Have you ever been to a music festival or concert?

2. What kind of music is best for exercising? How about relaxing?

3. Do you listen to music while you study? Why or why not?

Writing Practice

Write about your favorite musician. Try to answer these questions.

1. Who is your favorite musician or group?

2. What are your favorite songs?

3. Why do you like this music?

4. How does it make you feel?

5. Have you ever seen your favorite musician or group in a concert? If yes, when and how was it?

6. Describe the personality of this musician or the group's members.

UNIT 4

Sendai

 ## Guessing Twin Cities

Three of these cities are twinned with Sendai. Can you guess which ones?

Cities	Yes or No	Cities	Yes or No
Amsterdam, The Netherlands		Orlando, Florida, USA	
Copenhagen, Denmark		Oulu, Finland	
Gwangju, South Korea		Tainan, Taiwan	

Building-up Vocabulary

Match the words with the Japanese meanings from the box below.

English	Japanese	English	Japanese
interesting		research	
funny		mind	
seem like		elderly	
natural		field	

…のようである	心	おもしろい	年配の
自然な	…を研究する、研究	興味深い	分野

Reading Practice

Read the article below and then answer the comprehension questions.

Oulu

Oulu is the fifth largest city in Finland. It has a population of nearly 200,000 people. The city has a very interesting cultural life. There are many music festivals held every year in the city. This includes a huge rock festival held in the summer called Qstock. Since 1996, the Air Guitar World Championships has taken place in Oulu. This is a very famous and funny event and people come from all over the world to watch it. The city is also home to the Mieskuoro Huutajat, which means "Men's Choir Shouters." This is a chorus group that loudly shouts songs and it is famous for its unique musical style.

Performers at the Air Guitar Championships

Sendai and Oulu have been twin cities since 2005. Because they both have strong academic institutions and applied technology sectors, this seems like a natural partnership. Many new technologies are researched, developed, and tested in both cities. Both cities focus much of their research on the idea of wellness. This is the idea that human beings need more than just good physical health. They also need to have a life balance of mind, spirit, and body to be truly healthy. Much of the technology that has come from Oulu is used to help elderly people. The cities of Sendai and Oulu are working closely together in this field. Researchers from Sendai's universities participate in these kinds of projects together with Finnish scientists. This has helped to improve the quality of life for elderly Japanese.

---

choir「聖歌隊」 chorus「合唱」 loudly「大声で」 institution「機関」 applied technology「応用技術」 wellness「健康福祉」 human being「人間」 physical「肉体の」 truly「本当に」 Finnish「フィンランド人の」 quality「質」

UNIT 4   Sendai

Comprehension Questions

Read the sentences below about the article. Circle **T** for *True* or **F** for *False*.

1. Oulu is the biggest city in Finland. [T / F]
2. Qstock is a big annual rock festival held in Oulu. [T / F]
3. The Air Guitar World Championships started in 1996. [T / F]
4. Mieskuoro Huutajat means "Men's Choir Shouters." [T / F]
5. Oulu and Sendai have been twin cities since the previous century. [T / F]
6. Sendai and Oulu both have strong academic institutions. [T / F]
7. Wellness means the same as being in good physical health. [T / F]

Brainstorming

In a moment you will hear some facts about Sendai. First, brainstorm about Sendai. What do you know about Sendai?

Listening Practice

Listen to the facts about Sendai and fill in the blanks.

1. The Sendai Tanabata Festival is a large and _____ _____.
2. It _____ _____ everyone knows that grilled beef tongue is Sendai's _____ _____ dish.
3. The Hirose-gawa River _____ _____ the _____ of Sendai.
4. The _____ _____ in Sendai is Mount Funagata.
5. Sendai is sometimes called "The _____ _____ _____" mainly because it _____ _____ zelkova _____.
6. The _____ in Sendai are _____ _____ _____ for the Sendai Pageant of Starlight.
7. Tohoku University was _____ _____ Japanese university to accept female _____ _____ _____.

UNIT 4   Sendai

🌐 Working in a Group

Work with your group. Prepare some answers to these questions about a town or prefecture with a nickname that you know about.

1. What is the nickname? Which town or prefecture has it?

2. Why does the town or prefecture have that nickname?

3. Do you like it? Why or why not?

4. Do you know any other towns or prefectures with nicknames in Japan? If yes, what are they and what are their nicknames?

🌐 Writing Practice

Write about nicknames. Try to answer these questions.

1. Do you or your friends have nicknames? If yes, what is it (are they)?

2. Do you know any famous people with nicknames? If yes, who are they and what are their nicknames?

3. How did they get these nicknames?

4. What nickname would you like to have? Why?

5. Why do you think people give nicknames to others?

6. Is it always good to have a nickname? Why or why not?

UNIT 5

Tokyo

Guessing Twin Cities

Three of these places are twinned with Tokyo. Can you guess which ones?

Cities/States	Yes or No	Cities/States	Yes or No
Beijing, China		New York City, New York, USA	
Manchester, England		São Paulo, Brazil	
Mumbai, India		Washington, DC, USA	

Building-up Vocabulary

Match the words with the Japanese meanings from the box below.

English	Japanese	English	Japanese
state		serve	
include		wrap	
ethnically		distant	
affect		exhibit	

…に影響を及ぼす	（飲食物）を出す	…を包む	州
人種的に	離れた	展示会	…を含む

25

São Paulo

São Paulo is a state in southeast Brazil with about 44 million people. Over the last 150 years, many different people from around the world have immigrated to São Paulo. This includes Italians, Germans, Arabs, and Japanese. In fact, the city of São Paulo has the largest number of ethnically Japanese people living outside of Japan. The large number of Japanese living in São Paulo has strongly affected the local culture. Recently, Japanese food has become very popular among Brazilian people. Now, there are many Japanese restaurants. One kind of Japanese fast food restaurant is called a "temakeria." It serves a kind of hand-rolled sushi that is wrapped in something like seaweed.

São Paulo is a melting pot of many different people

Since 1990, Tokyo and the state of São Paulo have had a twin-city style of relationship. Although they are distant from each other, they have created many new exchanges over the years. Many universities in Tokyo and São Paulo have a student exchange program. There is also an art exchange. The Tokyo Fuji Art Museum, for example, has helped put on exhibits and performances that show the culture of both countries.

---

immigrate 「移住してくる」　seaweed 「海藻、海苔」　art museum 「美術館」　put on … 「…を催す」

UNIT 5 Tokyo

Comprehension Questions

Read the sentences below about the article. Circle **T** for *True* or **F** for *False*.

1. São Paulo is located in southwest Brazil. [T / F]
2. The state of São Paulo has a population of over 11 million people. [T / F]
3. The city of São Paulo has the smallest number of ethnically Japanese people living outside of Japan. [T / F]
4. Not many people in Brazil like Japanese food. [T / F]
5. Temakeria is a kind of hand-rolled sushi. [T / F]
6. Tokyo and São Paulo have been twin cities for about 150 years. [T / F]
7. A museum in Tokyo has helped put on some events showing Japanese and Brazilian culture. [T / F]

Brainstorming

In a moment you will hear some facts about Tokyo. First, brainstorm about Tokyo. What do you know about Tokyo?

Listening Practice

Listen to the facts about Tokyo and fill in the blanks.

1. The Kanto region includes Tokyo _____ _____ _____ _____ prefectures.
2. Tokyo has a population of _____ _____ _____ _____ people.
3. Ueno Park _____ _____ _____ with some well-known _____ .
4. The _____ Summer Olympics will _____ _____ _____ Tokyo.
5. Tokyo _____ _____ _____ _____ the Japanese government and the Imperial Palace.
6. Tokyo has _____ _____ economy _____ _____ _____ in the _____ in terms of GDP.
7. Tokyo has _____ professional _____ _____ .

UNIT 5 Tokyo

Working in a Group

Work with your group. Prepare some answers to these questions about city life.

1. What are some of the advantages of living in a city?

2. What are some of the disadvantages of living in a city?

3. What is your favorite city? Why?

4. What are some differences between living in the city and living in the country?

Writing Practice

Write about your dream home. Try to answer these questions.

1. Would you prefer to live in a house or an apartment? Why?

2. How many rooms would it have?

3. Who would you live with?

4. Would you prefer to live in the city or countryside? Why?

5. Would you have any special rooms?

6. Why do you want this kind of home?

UNIT 6

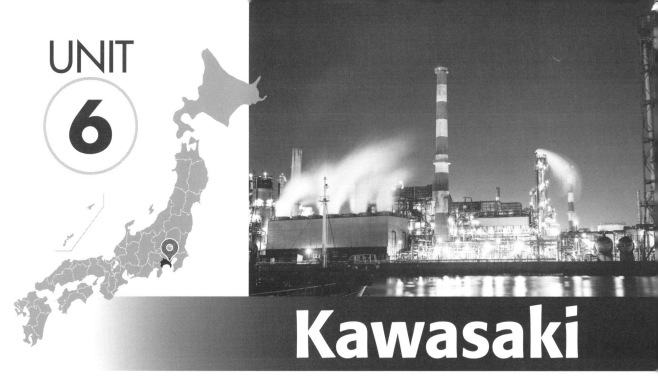

Kawasaki

Guessing Twin Cities

Three of these cities are twinned with Kawasaki. Can you guess which ones?

Cities	Yes or No	Cities	Yes or No
Baltimore, Maryland, USA		Salzburg, Austria	
Berlin, Germany		Sheffield, England	
Madrid, Spain		Sydney, Australia	

Building-up Vocabulary

Match the words with the Japanese meanings from the box below.

English	Japanese	English	Japanese
heritage		damage	
church		repair	
view		support	
composer		based	

景色	教会	…を修理する	…に被害を与える
援助	遺産	基づいた	作曲家

29

Reading Practice

Read the article below and then answer the comprehension questions.

Salzburg

Salzburg is a city in Austria famous for its beautiful buildings and musical importance. It is the fourth largest city in Austria, with a population of around 150,000. The Historic Center of the City of Salzburg has been a UNESCO World
5 Heritage Site since 1996. This site has many beautiful churches and towers. The view of Salzburg and its nearby mountains are incredible. You can also visit the house of Wolfgang Amadeus Mozart in this area
10 of the city. Salzburg was the birthplace and home to this world-famous composer. Mozart's sons and wife started the Mozarteum Orchestra Salzburg. This is the city's orchestra even today. It is among
15 the best symphony orchestras in all of Austria.

A picturesque view of Salzburg—the home of Mozart

Kawasaki and Salzburg are twin cities. On March 11, 2011, the Muza Kawasaki Symphony Hall was damaged during the Great East Japan Earthquake. The city of Salzburg donated 200,000 euros to help repair the hall. A monument
20 stands just outside the hall to thank Salzburg for its support. The bell at the top of the monument is a replica of the Salzburg Cathedral Bell. There are also some musical notes at the top of it. These are the notes to a Mozart score. The two cities have built a strong relationship based around friendship and music.

---

importance「重要性」 UNESCO「ユネスコ（国際連合教育科学文化機関）」 incredible「すばらしい」
the Great East Japan Earthquake「東日本大震災」 donate「寄付する」 replica「レプリカ、複製」
cathedral「大聖堂」 musical note「音符」 score「楽譜」

UNIT 6   Kawasaki

Comprehension Questions

Read the sentences below about the article. Circle **T** for *True* or **F** for *False*.

1. Salzburg is the second biggest city in Austria.   [T / F]
2. About 150,000 people live in Salzburg.   [T / F]
3. There are mountains near Salzburg.   [T / F]
4. You can visit Beethoven's house in this city.   [T / F]
5. The Muza Kawasaki Symphony Hall was damaged by a flood.   [T / F]
6. A monument stands outside the hall to thank Salzburg.   [T / F]
7. There are musical notes at the top of the monument.   [T / F]

Brainstorming

In a moment you will hear some facts about Kawasaki. First, brainstorm about Kawasaki. What do you know about Kawasaki?

Listening Practice

Listen to the facts about Kawasaki and fill in the blanks.

1. There is a _____ _____ of Kawasaki's factory zone at night.

2. Kawasaki has a population of _____ _____ _____ _____ .

3. Kawasaki Daishi is the _____ _____ _____ temple in the Kanto region.

4. There are many _____ barbecue _____ and _____ _____ markets in Korea Town.

5. People can go shopping _____ _____ _____ shopping spots in Kawasaki.

6. People _____ _____ _____ crafts at Ikuta Ryokuchi Park in Kawasaki.

7. One famous place in Ikuta Ryokuchi Park is _____ _____ of Fujiko F. Fujio, the creator of Doraemon.

UNIT 6   Kawasaki

Working in a Group

Work with your group. Prepare some answers to these questions about a shopping area that you know about.

1. What is the best place to shop?

2. What kinds of things can you buy there?

3. Why is it the best place to shop?

4. What are the top 3 stores in this shopping area?

5. Are they expensive to shop in?

Writing Practice

Write your feelings about shopping. Try to answer these questions.

1. Do you like shopping? Why or why not?

2. How often do you go shopping?

3. Do you prefer to go shopping with friends or alone? Why?

4. How much do you spend shopping each time you go?

5. Do you shop online? Why or why not?

6. When is the best time for you to go shopping?

UNIT 7

Kanazawa

Guessing Twin Cities

Three of these cities are twinned with Kanazawa. Can you guess which ones?

Cities	Yes or No	Cities	Yes or No
Brussels, Belgium		Los Angeles, California, USA	
Jeddah, Saudi Arabia		Nancy, France	
Jeonju, South Korea		Suzhou, China	

Building-up Vocabulary

Match the words with the Japanese meanings from the box below.

English	Japanese	English	Japanese
surround		souvenir	
experience		amazing	
widely		aspect	
throughout		tie	

…を体験する	…の隅から隅まで	驚嘆すべき	きずな
…を囲む	おみやげ	見方	広く

UNIT 7 Kanazawa

🌐 Reading Practice

Read the article below and then answer the comprehension questions.

Jeonju

Jeonju is a city located in the Honam region of South Korea. The city is surrounded by mountains. More than 650,000 people live in the city. There are many things to experience while visiting Jeonju. You can eat Jeonju-style *bibimbap*. This food is widely known throughout Korea. You may also be interested in
5 visiting a Hanok Village. Hanoks are traditional Korean houses. There are many small shops in which to buy souvenirs or drink tea. Jeonju's International Sori
10 Festival takes place each autumn. Visitors to the festival can hear lots of amazing traditional Korean and world music.

Enjoy traditional Korean music at a Hanok Village

Kanazawa and Jeonju became twin cities in 2002. Much like Kanazawa,
15 Jeonju is a very famous cultural center. One similarity that the two cities share is the making of traditional paper. Kanazawa is the capital of Ishikawa Prefecture, which is known throughout Japan for its *washi*. Jeonju's citizens are likewise very proud of their history of crafting Korean traditional paper called *hanji*. As a result, one aspect of their relationship is exchanging *washi* and *hanji*. There are also food
20 exchanges between the two cities and several *bibimbap* restaurants have recently opened in Kanazawa. The two cities are still working hard to create stronger ties through sports and music exchanges.

---

autumn 「秋」 likewise 「同じように」 be proud of ... 「…を誇りに思う」 craft 「手で…を作る」
as a result 「結果として」

Comprehension Questions

Read the sentences below about the article. Circle **T** for *True* or **F** for *False*.

1. Honam is the name of a region in South Korea. [T / F]
2. Jeonju-style *bibimbap* is not well-known in Korea. [T / F]
3. Hanoks are a type of traditional Korean house. [T / F]
4. Jeonju's International Sori Festival takes place each spring. [T / F]
5. Jeonju and Kanazawa became twin cities in 2012. [T / F]
6. Ishikawa Prefecture is known throughout Japan for its *hanji*. [T / F]
7. Kanazawa and Jeonju exchange *washi* and *hanji*. [T / F]

Brainstorming

In a moment you will hear some facts about Kanazawa. First, brainstorm about Kanazawa. What do you know about Kanazawa?

Listening Practice

Listen to the facts about Kanazawa and fill in the blanks.

1. Kanazawa was the center of the Maeda clan _____ _____ Edo period.

2. There are many _____ _____ _____ Kanazawa with old shrines and temples.

3. Terashima Kurando was a samurai and painter whose _____ _____ _____ Kanazawa Castle.

4. The weather in Kanazawa helps people make _____ _____ like rice, sweets, and sake.

5. The _____ _____ _____ _____ the Hakusan National Park, the Japanese Alps, and the Noto Peninsula National Park.

6. _____ _____ _____ big Japanese garden called Kenroku-en in Kanazawa.

7. Kanazawa _____ _____ _____ climate with heavy snow in the winter.

Working in a Group

Work with your group. Prepare some answers to these questions about an Edo-period clan that you know about.

1. What happened with the clan during this time?

2. Do you find this period of history interesting? Why or why not?

3. Who is a person from this time you find interesting? Why?

Writing Practice

Write about a person in history who you find interesting. Try to answer these questions.

1. Describe the person.

2. Why do you find him/her interesting?

3. What is his/her name?

4. What did he/she do?

5. Have you met him/her?

6. Why did you choose this person?

UNIT 8

Nagoya

Guessing Twin Cities

Three of these cities are twinned with Nagoya. Can you guess which ones?

Cities	Yes or No	Cities	Yes or No
Athens, Greece		Rome, Italy	
Los Angeles, California, USA		Sydney, Australia	
Mexico City, Mexico		Toronto, Canada	

Building-up Vocabulary

Match the words with the Japanese meanings from the box below.

English	Japanese	English	Japanese
variety		location	
geography		neighborhood	
valley		eager	
desert		sculpture	

地理	多種多様さ	地域、近隣住民	場所
谷	砂漠	熱望して	彫刻

37

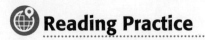

Reading Practice

Read the article below and then answer the comprehension questions.

Los Angeles

Los Angeles (or "L.A." as it is commonly called) is known around the world as the place where Hollywood movies originate. About 3.8 million people live in Los Angeles. Hollywood is a part of Los Angeles, where many famous movies and
5 television shows are made. L.A. is close to a great variety of geography such as mountains, valleys, and deserts. For this reason, it is perfect for film studios because they can quickly and easily film on many different kinds of locations. Los Angeles
10 is also famous for its many highways. Because the city is so huge, most people use a car or bus to get around. Los Angeles is a city of great variety. People from over 140 countries live in the city. It is a big mix of lifestyles, neighborhoods, and
15 cultures.

Welcome to Hollywood!

Los Angeles and Nagoya have a very close bond as twin cities. People from both cities are eager to share with and learn about each other. Los Angeles regularly sends its students and teachers to Nagoya on a cultural exchange program. Los Angeles often displays art created by children in Nagoya. Both cities
20 also give each other gifts. Nagoya presented a portable shrine, a tea house, and a clock tower to Los Angeles. In return, Los Angeles has given beautiful sculptures to Nagoya. These are on display in Los Angeles Square in Nagoya's Hisaya Odori Park.

---

commonly「一般に」 originate「発祥する」 a great variety of …「非常にさまざまな…」
film「映画、…を撮影する」 highway「幹線道路」 mix「混合」 lifestyle「生活様式」 regularly「定期的に」
portable shrine「みこし」 clock tower「時計塔」 in return「お返しに」

UNIT 8 Nagoya

Comprehension Questions

Read the sentences below about the article. Circle **T** for *True* or **F** for *False*.

1. Los Angeles is sometimes called "Los." [T / F]
2. Los Angeles is a part of Hollywood. [T / F]
3. There is only desert near Los Angeles. [T / F]
4. There are many highways in Los Angeles. [T / F]
5. People from Los Angeles and Nagoya are interested in learning about each other. [T / F]
6. Nagoya presented a large park to Los Angeles. [T / F]
7. Los Angeles has given sculptures to Nagoya. [T / F]

Brainstorming

In a moment you will hear some facts about Nagoya. First, brainstorm about Nagoya. What do you know about Nagoya?

Listening Practice

Listen to the facts about Nagoya and fill in the blanks.

1. There are only three cities in Japan _____ _____ Nagoya.
2. Higashiyama Zoo _____ _____ _____ _____ largest zoos _____ _____.
3. Nagoya is _____ _____ _____ many cat cafés.
4. The port of Nagoya is the largest in Japan _____ _____ shipping.
5. The Nagoya TV Tower was destroyed _____ _____ Godzilla _____.
6. Nagoya Castle is one of the city's _____ _____ _____.
7. Nagoya is well-known for its delicious grilled eel _____ _____ steamed rice.

UNIT 8　Nagoya

Working in a Group

Work with your group. Prepare some answers to these questions about a popular restaurant that you know about.

1. What is the most famous restaurant?

2. What kinds of food can you eat there?

3. How much does an average dish cost?

4. Have you been there? If yes, how many times?

5. Do you like it? Why or why not?

Writing Practice

Write about cooking. Try to answer these questions.

1. How often do you cook?

2. Are you good at cooking?

3. What are some things that you can cook?

4. What dish are you best at cooking?

5. What is the easiest dish to cook?

6. Who is the best cook you know?

UNIT 9

Kyoto

🌐 Guessing Twin Cities

Three of these cities are twinned with Kyoto City. Can you guess which ones?

Cities	Yes or No	Cities	Yes or No
Cancun, Mexico		Kiev, Ukraine	
Florence, Italy		London, England	
Johannesburg, South Africa		Paris, France	

🌐 Building-up Vocabulary

Match the words with the Japanese meanings from the box below.

English	Japanese	English	Japanese
theater		vegetable	
often		available	
appear		association	
cheap		recognize	

劇場	協会	頻繁に	入手できる
出演する	野菜	安い	…を認識する

41

UNIT 9   Kyoto

Reading Practice

Read the article below and then answer the comprehension questions.

Kiev

Kiev is the capital city of Ukraine. Almost three million people live there. It has an interesting culture and history. Kiev is famous for its world-class theater. Ballet and opera stars from around the world often appear on stage at the Kiev Opera House. There are many other theaters throughout the city and tickets to see some shows are surprisingly cheap. Many beautiful churches can be found in Kiev. If you visit St. Sophia's Cathedral or St. Michael's Monastery, you can learn about the history and culture of this famous city. The golden domes of the cathedrals and churches can be seen from almost anywhere in Kiev.

St. Michael's Monastery graced with its golden domes

Visitors can also try many kinds of Ukranian food. Borscht is a kind of vegetable soup. There are many varieties of borscht and you can try almost all of them in Kiev! Ukranian pies and fish are also available in Kiev and they are delicious.

Kiev and Kyoto City have been twin cities since 1971. There is a park called "Kyoto Park" in Kiev. It is a Japanese-style park with rock gardens, a five-meter stone pagoda, and hundreds of cherry blossom trees. In addition, the Kyoto Ikebana Association sometimes holds flower exhibitions in Kiev and its other sister cities. Both cities are recognized around the world for their cultural importance. Both cities also have world-famous ballet performers and groups.

---

surprisingly 「驚くほど」　monastery 「修道院」　borscht 「ボルシチ（ロシアのビート入りスープ）」
in addition 「加えて」

UNIT 9   Kyoto

Comprehension Questions

Read the sentences below about the article. Circle **T** for *True* or **F** for *False*.

1. Kiev is located in the country of Poland.   [T / F]
2. Kiev is well-known for its world-class theater.   [T / F]
3. It is always very expensive to go to the theater in Kiev.   [T / F]
4. The domes of the Kiev cathedrals are red.   [T / F]
5. Borscht is a kind of meat pie.   [T / F]
6. Kiev and Kyoto City have been twin cities for over 45 years.   [T / F]
7. Kiev and Kyoto are not culturally important cities.   [T / F]

Brainstorming

In a moment you will hear some facts about Kyoto City/Prefecture. First, brainstorm about Kyoto. What do you know about Kyoto?

Listening Practice

Listen to the facts about Kyoto and fill in the blanks.

1. Maiko can _____ _____ _____ in the Gion district in Kyoto City.
2. Kyoto is the _____ _____ to enjoy *shojin ryori*, _____ _____ _____ vegetarian cuisine, in Japan.
3. Nishiki Market is a _____ _____ _____ with over 100 shops.
4. Kyoto has _____ _____ Buddhist temples and Shinto shrines.
5. The Golden Pavilion at Kinkaku-ji was _____ _____ the _____ century.
6. There is a beautiful _____ _____ _____ _____ from Kiyomizu-dera.
7. The _____ _____ of Kyoto City was Heiankyo, or Capital of Peace.

UNIT 9   **Kyoto**

🌐 Working in a Group

Work with your group. Prepare some answers to these questions about things to see and do in Kyoto.

1. Have you ever been to Kyoto? If yes, what did you like the most?

   _____

2. What are some of the most popular tourist destinations in Kyoto?

   _____

3. When is the best time to visit Kyoto? Why?

   _____

4. What delicious food can people eat there?

   _____

5. What is a typical souvenir from Kyoto?

   _____

🌐 Writing Practice

Write about a dream vacation. Try to answer these questions.

1. Where would you like to go?

   _____

2. Who would you go with?

   _____

3. How much would it cost?

   _____

4. How long would you stay?

   _____

5. What kind of place would you stay in?

   _____

6. Why would you choose this place?

   _____

UNIT 10

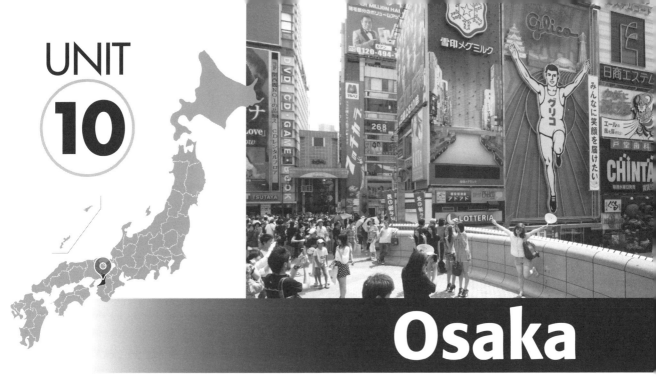

Osaka

🌐 Guessing Twin Cities

Three of these cities are twinned with Osaka City. Can you guess which ones?

Cities	Yes or No	Cities	Yes or No
Chicago, Illinois, USA		Ottawa, Canada	
Lima, Peru		Saint Petersburg, Russia	
Melbourne, Australia		Singapore, Singapore	

🌐 Building-up Vocabulary

Match the words with the Japanese meanings from the box below.

English	Japanese	English	Japanese
capital		perfect	
industry		atmosphere	
feature film		along	
historical		whole	

全体の	…に沿って	申し分のない	歴史的な
首都	雰囲気	産業	長編映画

45

UNIT 10 Osaka

Reading Practice

Read the article below and then answer the comprehension questions.

Melbourne

Melbourne is the cultural capital of Australia. It has a population of over four million people. It is located in the southeast of Australia. Melbourne is the home of Australia's film and television industry. In fact, this is where the world's first feature film was made in 1906. This long historical association with films
5 and movies makes Melbourne the perfect place for an international film festival. The Melbourne International Film Festival is held every year. The city also has many other kinds of international festivals such as a
10 comedy festival and an arts festival. Although the weather in Melbourne can change quickly, the city has a pleasant atmosphere. Many events are held along the city's waterfront.

Many interesting events are held in this city down under

15 Melbourne and Osaka City have been twin cities since 1978. To celebrate their close relationship, the Melbourne Osaka Cup is held approximately every four years. This is a yacht race from Melbourne to Osaka. It is a very famous event. People call it "The Race." The Osaka Festival is held annually in Melbourne. It is a big festival where Australians can enjoy watching Japanese performances. They
20 can also eat Japanese food and try some traditional Japanese dances. It is great fun for the whole family!

---

in fact 「実際は」 waterfront 「臨海部」 annually 「毎年」

UNIT 10 Osaka

Comprehension Questions

Read the sentences below about the article. Circle **T** for *True* or **F** for *False*.

1. Melbourne is the capital of Australia. [T / F]
2. The world's first feature film was made in Melbourne. [T / F]
3. Melbourne's film festival takes place every year. [T / F]
4. It is always hot and sunny in Melbourne. [T / F]
5. Melbourne and Osaka City have been twin cities since 1906. [T / F]
6. The Melbourne Osaka Cup takes place annually. [T / F]
7. People can try Japanese food at the Osaka Festival. [T / F]

Brainstorming

In a moment you will hear some facts about Osaka City/Prefecture. First, brainstorm about Osaka. What do you know about Osaka?

Listening Practice

Listen to the facts about Osaka and fill in the blanks.

1. The big Glico running man sign _____ _____ _____ _____ of Osaka.

2. Universal Studios Japan is a famous _____ _____ located in Osaka.

3. Osaka Prefecture is the _____ _____ prefecture in Japan.

4. Osaka Castle was constructed _____ _____ by Toyotomi Hideyoshi.

5. Osaka was _____ _____ Naniwa until the _____ century.

6. Dotonbori is _____ _____ _____ Osaka City where tourists _____ _____ *takoyaki*, *kushikatsu*, and _____ _____ _____ great food.

7. Osaka has _____ _____ kilometers of subway track, _____ _____ _____ Japan.

UNIT 10 Osaka

🌐 Working in a Group

Work with your group. Prepare some answers to these questions about a famous amusement park that you know about.

1. What is the best amusement park you have ever visited? Why?

2. What was your favorite ride or activity? Why?

3. Were there any rides or activities you didn't like? Why?

4. Was the amusement park expensive?

🌐 Writing Practice

Write about an amusement park you would like to visit. Try to answer these questions.

1. Where would you like to go?

2. Who would you like to go with?

3. When would you like to go there?

4. What would you do there?

5. How would you get there?

6. Why would you like to go there?

UNIT 11

Kobe

Guessing Twin Cities

Three of these cities are twinned with Kobe. Can you guess which ones?

Cities	Yes or No	Cities	Yes or No
Barcelona, Spain		Istanbul, Turkey	
Bogotá, Colombia		Riyadh, Saudi Arabia	
Brisbane, Australia		Seattle, Washington, USA	

Building-up Vocabulary

Match the words with the Japanese meanings from the box below.

English	Japanese	English	Japanese
cargo		sightseeing	
rest		in common	
surroundings		hill	
welcome		wear	

…を着る	貨物	共通して	環境
丘	残り	…を歓迎する	観光

49

UNIT 11 Kobe

Reading Practice

Read the article below and then answer the comprehension questions.

Seattle

Seattle's Space Needle reaches sky-high

Seattle is a major port city in the northwest United States. It is a major city in the state of Washington. Each year, millions of tons of cargo pass through the port of
5 Seattle on its way to and from Japan and the rest of Asia. It is a city famous for its delicious coffee, relaxed lifestyle, and beautiful natural surroundings. Over 600,000 people live in Seattle and it welcomes almost 20 million
10 visitors each year. Popular sightseeing places include Seattle's famous Space Needle, Pike Place Fish Market, and the 92-acre Woodland Park Zoo.

Seattle and Kobe have been twin cities since 1957. Kobe was the first city
15 to become Seattle's twin. The two cities have many kinds of cultural, educational, and business exchanges. The cities have a lot in common. They both have a similar geography and they are both important port cities. The two cities have had many student and teacher exchanges over the years. They have also given each other many gifts. The cherry trees in Seattle's Kobe Terrace Park are a gift from the
20 people of Kobe. There is also a 200-year-old *yukimidoro* stone lantern at the top of a hill in the park. Seattle holds an annual Cherry Blossom Festival where people can learn about Japanese culture, wear a kimono, and enjoy some great *taiko* drumming performances.

---

on one's way「途中で」 fish market「魚市場」 acre「エーカー(面積の単位)」 stone lantern「石灯籠」

UNIT 11   Kobe

Comprehension Questions

Read the sentences below about the article. Circle **T** for *True* or **F** for *False*.

1. Seattle is a port city in the northwest United States.   [T / F]
2. Seattle is located in the state of Washington.   [T / F]
3. About 60,000 people live in Seattle.   [T / F]
4. One popular sightseeing place in Seattle is the Space Needle.   [T / F]
5. Kobe was the first city to be twinned with Seattle.   [T / F]
6. The people of Seattle gave Kobe cherry blossom trees.   [T / F]
7. The Cherry Blossom Festival is an annual event in Seattle.   [T / F]

Brainstorming

In a moment you will hear some facts about Kobe. First, brainstorm about Kobe. What do you know about Kobe?

Listening Practice

🎧 34

Listen to the facts about Kobe and fill in the blanks.

1. The Kobe Steel Kobelco Steelers _____ _____ _____ Top League rugby champions.

2. The annual Kobe Marathon is _____ _____ _____ victims of earthquakes and other disasters.

3. Kobe is most famous for its Kobe _____ and Arima _____ _____.

4. Kobe Golf Club was Japan's _____ _____ _____.

5. Kobe _____ _____ _____ _____ much of the Studio Ghibli film, *Grave of the Fireflies*.

6. The Kobe Sports Park _____ _____ _____ _____ to play sports and watch events.

7. Kobe was one of the _____ _____ of the _____ FIFA World Cup.

51

UNIT 11   Kobe

🌐 Working in a Group

Work with your group. Prepare some answers to these questions about a sports event you have seen.

1. What was the name of that event?

2. What sports were played at that event?

3. When and where did it take place?

4. Who were some of the most famous players of this sport?

5. Did you go to that event or watch it on TV?

🌐 Writing Practice

Write your feelings about your favorite sport. Try to answer these questions.

1. Do you play any sports? If yes, what do you play? If not, what would you like to play?

2. Do you like to exercise? Why or why not?

3. Are you a member of any sports team? If not, have you ever been?

4. Is this sport popular?

5. Do your friends play this sport?

6. When did you start playing this sport?

UNIT 12
Hiroshima

Guessing Twin Cities

Three of these cities are twinned with Hiroshima City. Can you guess which ones?

Cities	Yes or No	Cities	Yes or No
Auckland, New Zealand		Hanover, Germany	
Daegu, South Korea		Honolulu, Hawaii, USA	
Geneva, Switzerland		Liverpool, England	

Building-up Vocabulary

Match the words with the Japanese meanings from the box below.

English	Japanese	English	Japanese
native		temple	
settle		competition	
sheltered		personal	
solid		representative	

個人的な	先住の	寺	…に移り住む
保護された	代表者	堅実な	試合

Reading Practice

Read the article below and then answer the comprehension questions.

Honolulu

Honolulu is the state capital of Hawaii. It has been the capital of the Hawaiian Islands since 1845. The city also has the largest population of any city in Hawaii. The city of Honolulu has a population of about 390,000 people. It is approximately 6,210 kilometers from Tokyo. A flight from Tokyo usually takes just over seven hours. The native people of Hawaii are thought to have settled there around 1200. The first European to visit Honolulu was Captain William Brown. He landed in Honolulu in 1794. The name Honolulu means sheltered harbor or calm port.

World-famous Waikiki beach is truly a paradise

Since 1959, Honolulu and Hiroshima City have been twin cities. Their relationship is very solid. This is partly because of their common history. In the 19th century, about 10,000 people from Hiroshima came to live in Hawaii. If you visit Honolulu, it is easy to see the influence of Japanese culture in the city and throughout the Hawaiian Islands. There are Japanese temples and many people can speak fluent Japanese. Each November, the city of Hiroshima has a "Honolulu Day." There are also friendly competitions between university baseball teams from both cities. Hiroshima City has also held special photo exhibits in Honolulu to share personal experiences of the atomic bombing in 1945. Honolulu has also sent representatives to Hiroshima City to attend the Peace Memorial Ceremony held every August 6th.

---

harbor 「港」　calm 「穏やかな」　fluent 「流暢な」　atomic bombing 「原爆投下」　memorial ceremony 「記念式典」

UNIT 12 Hiroshima

Comprehension Questions

Read the sentences below about the article. Circle **T** for *True* or **F** for *False*.

1. Honolulu is the capital of the state of Hawaii. [T / F]
2. About 390,000 people live in Honolulu. [T / F]
3. Honolulu is 1,200 kilometers from Japan. [T / F]
4. The first European visited Honolulu in 1974. [T / F]
5. In the 19th century, 10,000 people from Hiroshima came to Hawaii. [T / F]
6. Each December, the city of Hiroshima has a "Honolulu Day." [T / F]
7. Representatives from Honolulu have attended the Peace Memorial Ceremony in Hiroshima. [T / F]

Brainstorming

In a moment you will hear some facts about Hiroshima City/Prefecture. First, brainstorm about Hiroshima. What do you know about Hiroshima?

Listening Practice

🎧 37

Listen to the facts about Hiroshima and fill in the blanks.

1. Hiroshima City is _____ _____ _____ in the Chugoku and Shikoku _____.
2. Hiroshima Prefecture is connected to Ehime Prefecture _____ _____ _____ _____ the Seto Inland Sea.
3. Hiroshima City _____ _____ _____ the Hiroshima Toyo Carp.
4. _____ _____ _____ _____ Japan's oysters come from Hiroshima Prefecture.
5. Hiroshima City holds an animated _____ _____ every two years.
6. The Hiroshima Peace Memorial Park _____ _____ _____ the center of Hiroshima City.
7. Hiroshima City's streetcar service _____ _____ _____ _____.

UNIT 12 Hiroshima

🌐 Working in a Group

Work with your group. Make a seven-day menu of your favorite food. Write a different food for each day.

Day	Meal (Breakfast, Lunch, or Dinner)
Monday	
Tuesday	
Wednesday	
Thursday	
Friday	
Saturday	
Sunday	

🌐 Writing Practice

Write about a restaurant you would like to visit. Try to answer these questions.

1. Where would you like to go?

   _____

2. Who would you like to go with?

   _____

3. When would you like to go there?

   _____

4. What would you like to eat there?

   _____

5. How much does it cost?

   _____

6. Why would you like to go there?

   _____

UNIT 13

Kochi

Guessing Twin Cities

Three of these cities are twinned with Kochi City. Can you guess which ones?

Cities	Yes or No	Cities	Yes or No
Brest, France		Surabaya, Indonesia	
Dublin, Ireland		Warsaw, Poland	
Fresno, California, USA		Wuhu, China	

Building-up Vocabulary

Match the words with the Japanese meanings from the box below.

English	Japanese	English	Japanese
purchase		outlook	
sort		benefit	
goods		participate	
arrive		vital	

商品	眺め、展望	きわめて重要な	利益を得る
到着する	参加する	…を購入する	種類

Reading Practice

Read the article below and then answer the comprehension questions.

Surabaya

Surabaya is a city of nearly three million people located on Java Island in Indonesia. It is the second largest city in Indonesia. Surabaya is known for its great shopping and big port. There are many shopping malls in Surabaya. The city is very popular with tourists for this reason. Visitors can purchase all sorts of goods
5 from around the world. This is because Surabaya is a major port city. The nearby port is called Tanjung Perak. It is one of the busiest ports in Indonesia. Many people and goods arrive through this port. As a result, the city has a very modern and international outlook. People speak Javanese in Surabaya although you can
10 also hear many other languages being spoken such as Chinese languages. Students come from many countries to attend Surabaya's universities and technical schools.

A wide variety of goods brings shoppers to Surabaya

15 Kochi City has been twinned with Surabaya since 1997. Both cities understood they could benefit economically and culturally from becoming twin cities. Kochi has a famous annual festival called the Yosakoi Festival. The Yosakoi-Remo Festival takes place in Surabaya. This festival celebrates the two cities' twin relationship. Yosakoi is a traditional dance that started in Kochi City while
20 Remo is Surabaya's traditional dance. Students from Kochi City sometimes visit Surabaya to participate in and watch this festival. Both cities have also benefitted from this relationship in other ways. Kochi imports lots of organic fertilizer, sugar, and sweet potatoes from Surabaya each year. This cultural and trade relationship is vital for Kochi City and all of Japan.

---

technical school「専門学校」 while「…であるけれども、一方では…」 import「…を輸入する」
organic fertilizer「有機肥料」

UNIT 13   Kochi

Comprehension Questions

Read the sentences below about the article. Circle **T** for *True* or **F** for *False*.

1. Surabaya is located on Java Island. [T / F]
2. Surabaya is popular because of its shopping malls. [T / F]
3. The nearby port is called Surabaya Port. [T / F]
4. Everyone speaks Japanese in Surabaya. [T / F]
5. Surabaya and Kochi City have been twin cities since 1997. [T / F]
6. Yosakoi is a traditional dance from Kochi. [T / F]
7. Kochi imports sugar and sweet potatoes from Surabaya. [T / F]

Brainstorming

In a moment you will hear some facts about Kochi City/Prefecture. First, brainstorm about Kochi. What do you know about Kochi?

Listening Practice

Listen to the facts about Kochi and fill in the blanks.

1. _____ _____ _____ many vegetables and fruit at the Kochi Sunday Market.

2. In Kochi Prefecture, *katsuo-no-tataki* _____ _____ _____ over a straw fire.

3. The most famous festival in Kochi City is the Yosakoi _____ _____ _____ _____ _____.

4. People wear _____ _____ _____ different costumes at the Yosakoi Festival.

5. Fishing and forestry _____ _____ _____ Kochi Prefecture's economy.

6. Kochi Castle is one of the city's _____ _____ _____.

7. The actress Ryoko Hirosue _____ _____ _____ Kochi City.

Working in a Group

Work with your group. Prepare some answers to these questions about movies.

1. How often do you watch movies?

2. How often do you go to the movie theater?

3. How often do you rent DVDs?

4. What sorts of movies do you like?

5. Are there any kinds of movies you dislike? If yes, what kinds and why?

Writing Practice

Write about your favorite actor or actress. Try to answer these questions.

1. Who is your favorite actor or actress?

2. Why do you like him/her?

3. What sorts of movies has he/she been in?

4. What are the names of the movies he/she has starred in?

5. Which ones have you seen?

6. What would you say to him/her if you met?

UNIT 14

Fukuoka

Guessing Twin Cities

Three of these cities are twinned with Fukuoka City. Can you guess which ones?

Cities	Yes or No	Cities	Yes or No
Auckland, New Zealand		Ipoh, Malaysia	
Bordeaux, France		Lima, Peru	
Cairo, Egypt		Oslo, Norway	

Building-up Vocabulary

Match the words with the Japanese meanings from the box below.

English	Japanese	English	Japanese
region		produce	
connect		feature	
indeed		collaboration	
grow		promote	

…を生産する	…を促進する	…を栽培する、発展する	実際に
共同制作	…を呼び物にする	…を関係させる	地方

Reading Practice

Read the article below and then answer the comprehension questions.

Bordeaux

Bordeaux is a city in the southwest of France. It is the ninth largest city in France. Bordeaux is the center of the Bordeaux region which is called Bordeaux Métropole in French. Over 700,000 people inhabit this area and many of them are connected to the wine-making industry. Bordeaux is very famous for its wine.

5 Wine-making is an old tradition in Bordeaux. In fact, people have been making wine in Bordeaux for more than 2,000 years. Indeed, Bordeaux produces some of the world's best wines. It is also the largest wine
10 growing area in France. More than 700 million bottles of Bordeaux wine are produced every year. Some of these are the most expensive and prestigious wines.

Harvesting grapes for top-grade wines

15 Fukuoka City and Bordeaux became twin cities in 1982. As port cities known for their universities, Fukuoka and Bordeaux share much in common with each other. The friendship between the cities has grown through university exchange programs and special events. Bordeaux wines are featured in many of Fukuoka's restaurants during the city's wine festivals. There have also been
20 artist exchanges and collaborations between the cities. For example, French and Japanese manga artists have worked together to promote tourism. Bordeaux has affectionately named one of its trams "Ville de Fukuoka," which means "City of Fukuoka"!

---

inhabit「…に住む」 prestigious「名声のある」 tourism「観光事業」 affectionately「愛情を込めて」

Comprehension Questions

Read the sentences below about the article. Circle **T** for *True* or **F** for *False*.

1. Bordeaux is the fifth largest city in France. [T / F]
2. Over 700,000 people live in Bordeaux Métropole. [T / F]
3. Beer-making is an old tradition in Bordeaux. [T / F]
4. Bordeaux produces more than 700 million bottles of beer. [T / F]
5. Fukuoka and Bordeaux have nothing in common with each other. [T / F]
6. Many of Fukuoka's restaurants feature Bordeaux wines during the city's wine festivals. [T / F]
7. Bordeaux has named one of their ships after Fukuoka. [T / F]

Brainstorming

In a moment you will hear some facts about Fukuoka City/Prefecture. First, brainstorm about Fukuoka. What do you know about Fukuoka?

Listening Practice

Listen to the facts about Fukuoka and fill in the blanks.

1. A big _____ _____ called Tenjin is _____ _____ _____ _____ Fukuoka City.
2. The Fukuoka Softbank Hawks _____ _____ _____ _____ every year.
3. Many new companies in Fukuoka _____ _____ _____ the smartphone business.
4. The tallest building in Fukuoka is called Fukuoka Tower, which is _____ _____ _____.
5. People in Fukuoka love eating at the food stalls _____ _____ _____ _____ _____.
6. It is _____ _____ _____ anywhere in Kyushu from Fukuoka _____ _____.
7. _____ _____ _____ that Fukuoka has the best *ramen* in Japan.

UNIT 14 Fukuoka

 Working in a Group

Work with your group. Prepare answers to these questions about your mobile phone.

1. How often do you use your phone?

2. When is the right age to get your first phone? Why?

3. What are some examples of good phone "manners"?

4. What are some good apps or sites for learning English?

 Writing Practice

Write about your phone or laptop. Try to answer these questions.

1. How important is your phone/laptop for your daily life?

2. What kind of things do you use your phone/laptop for?

3. How would you feel if you couldn't use your phone/laptop for a week?

4. Do you think you use your phone/laptop too much? Why or why not?

5. What kind of problems can people have if they use their phone/laptop too much?

UNIT 15

Kumamoto

🌐 Guessing Twin Cities

Three of these cities are twinned with Kumamoto City. Can you guess which ones?

Cities	Yes or No	Cities	Yes or No
Guilin, China		Rome, Italy	
Heidelberg, Germany		San Antonio, Texas, USA	
Lisbon, Portugal		Taipei, Taiwan	

🌐 Building-up Vocabulary

Match the words with the Japanese meanings from the box below.

English	Japanese	English	Japanese
site		garden	
develop		youth	
expert		friendly	
build		find out	

…を造る	若者	知る、理解する	…を発達させる
庭園	友好的な、親善の	専門家	（事件や事業が）行われた場所

Reading Practice

Read the article below and then answer the comprehension questions.

San Antonio

San Antonio is a city in the state of Texas in the southern United States. It has a population of over 1.4 million people. It is a very fast-growing city with a strong economy. The city is also known for its history. The Alamo is a
5 fortress that was the site of a famous battle in 1836. It is now a World Heritage Site and a museum. The city is very nice because of its scenery, especially along the San Antonio
10 River. For this reason, San Antonio is also called "River City."

The Alamo is Texas' most visited historic landmark

San Antonio and Kumamoto City are very active in developing their twin city relationship. The two cities have been twins since 1987. In 1989, Kumamoto City sent Japanese gardeners and experts to San Antonio. They built a beautiful
15 Japanese-style garden called "Kumamoto-en" in San Antonio's Botanical Gardens. Each year, the two cities celebrate their relationship in the garden. There have also been sports exchanges between the two cities. Kumamoto has sent youths to the city for a friendly baseball game. San Antonio has sent runners to compete in the Kumamoto Castle Marathon. There is also an annual festival called the
20 "Aki Matsuri" in San Antonio. Visitors can have fun finding out about Japan, participating in cosplay, watching sumo, and enjoying Japanese storytelling.

---

fast-growing 「急成長している」 fortress 「要塞地」 gardener 「庭師」 storytelling 「読み聞かせ」

UNIT 15 Kumamoto

Comprehension Questions

Read the sentences below about the article. Circle **T** for *True* or **F** for *False*.

1. San Antonio is the name of a state in America. [T / F]
2. The city is known for its rainy weather. [T / F]
3. The Alamo is a fortress that was the site of a battle. [T / F]
4. San Antonio is also known as "River City." [T / F]
5. San Antonio and Kumamoto City have been twin cities since 1936. [T / F]
6. "Kumamoto-en" is the name of a garden in San Antonio. [T / F]
7. There is an annual festival in San Antonio called "Yuki Matsuri." [T / F]

Brainstorming

In a moment you will hear some facts about Kumamoto City/Prefecture. First, brainstorm about Kumamoto. What do you know about Kumamoto?

Listening Practice

🎧 46

Listen to the facts about Kumamoto and fill in the blanks.

1. Kumamoto City has a population _____ _____ _____ people.

2. Suizenji is a _____ _____ _____ in Kumamoto City.

3. Lafcadio Hearn or Koizumi Yakumo lived in Kumamoto City and _____ _____ _____ _____.

4. Wood, stone, and plaster were _____ _____ _____ Kumamoto Castle.

5. A _____ _____ _____ from Kumamoto Prefecture is *basashi* or raw horse meat.

6. Eiichiro Oda, _____ _____ _____ *One Piece*, _____ _____ Kumamoto City.

7. Kumamoto Prefecture _____ _____ _____ mascot _____ Kumamon.

UNIT 15 Kumamoto

🌐 Working in a Group

Work with your group. Prepare some answers to these questions about famous authors that you know about.

1. Who is the most famous writer in Japan?

2. What books or comics did he/she write?

3. Have you read any of them? If yes, how did you feel about it/them? If not, which one(s) would you like to read?

4. Who is the most famous writer from a foreign country?

5. What books or comics did he/she write?

6. Have you read any of them? If yes, how did you feel about it/them? If not, which one(s) would you like to read?

🌐 Writing Practice

Write about your favorite book or comic. Try to answer these questions.

1. What is your favorite book or comic?

2. Why do you like it?

3. How many times have you read it?

4. Who is the author?

5. What happens in this story?

Glossary

このリストには、各ユニットの Reading Practice 本文で使われている重要語句とその本文のページ番号を収録しています。ただし、語注内の固有名詞は除外しています。

※ Building-up Vocabulary で取り上げている語句は太字で示し、語注で取り上げている語句はページ番号のあとに G を付けています。両方で取り上げている語句については、それぞれのユニットの本文のページ番号を収録しています。

名：名詞（句）　動：動詞（句）　形：形容詞（句）　副：副詞（句）　接：接続詞　前：前置詞

A

a great variety of ... 形 非常にさまざまな…	38G
acre 名 エーカー（面積の単位）	50G
affect 動 …に影響を及ぼす	26
affectionately 副 愛情を込めて	62G
along 前 …に沿って	46
amazing 形 驚嘆すべき	34
annually 副 毎年	46G
appear 動 出演する	42
applied technology 名 応用技術	22G
arrive 動 到着する	58
art museum 名 美術館	26G
as a result 副 結果として	34G
aspect 名 見方	34
association 名 協会	42
atmosphere 名 雰囲気	46
atomic bombing 名 原爆投下	54G
attend 動 (学校に)通う	14
autumn 名 秋	34G
available 形 入手できる	42

B

based 形 基づいた	30
be proud of ... 形 …を誇りに思う	34G
benefit 動 利益を得る	58
bloom 動 (花が)咲く	14
bond 名 きずな	10
build 動 …を造る	66

C

calm 形 穏やかな	54G
capital 名 首都	46
cargo 名 貨物	50
cathedral 名 大聖堂	30G
celebrate 動 …を祝う	10

cheap 形 安い	42
cherry blossom 名 サクラの花	14G
choir 名 聖歌隊	22G
chorus 名 合唱	22G
church 名 教会	30
citizen 名 市民	18
clock tower 名 時計塔	38G
collaboration 名 共同制作	62
commonly 副 一般に	38G
competition 名 試合	54
composer 名 作曲家	30
connect 動 …を関係させる	62
cooperation 名 協力	14G
craft 動 手で…を作る	34G

D

damage 動 …に被害を与える	30
desert 名 砂漠	38
develop 動 …を発達させる	66
distant 形 離れた	26
donate 動 寄付する	30G

E

eager 形 熱望して	38
elderly 形 年配の	22
entry 名 参加	10
ethnically 副 人種的に	26
exhibit 名 展示会	26
experience 動 …を体験する	34
expert 名 専門家	66

F

fast-growing 形 急成長している	66G
feature 動 …を呼び物にする	62
feature film 名 長編映画	46

69

field 名 分野	22
film 名 映画 動 …を撮影する	38G
find out 動 知る、理解する	66
Finnish 形 フィンランド人の	22G
fish market 名 魚市場	50G
fluent 形 流暢な	54G
folk 形 民間の	10G
fortress 名 要塞地	66G
friendly 形 友好的な、親善の	66
funny 形 おもしろい	22

G

garden 名 庭園	66
gardener 名 庭師	66G
geography 名 地理	38
goods 名 商品	58
grow 動 …を栽培する、発展する	62

H

harbor 名 港	54G
heritage 名 遺産	30
highway 名 幹線道路	38G
hill 名 丘	50
historical 形 歴史的な	46
hold 動 …を催す	10G
host 動 …を主催する	18
human being 名 人間	22G

I

immigrate 動 移住してくる	26G
import 動 …を輸入する	58G
importance 名 重要性	30G
in addition 副 加えて	42G
in common 副 共通して	50
in fact 副 実際は	46G
in honor of ... 副 …に敬意を表して	10G
in return 副 お返しに	38G
include 動 …を含む	26
incredible 形 すばらしい	30G
indeed 副 実際に	62
industry 名 産業	46
influence 名 影響	14
information 名 情報	14
inhabit 動 …に住む	62G
institution 名 機関	22G
interest in ... 名 …に対する興味	18G

interesting 形 興味深い	22

L

last 動 続く	10
lifestyle 名 生活様式	38G
likewise 副 同じように	34G
location 名 場所	38
loudly 副 大声で	22G

M

major 形 主要な	14
manufacturer 名 製造業者	18
marriage 名 結婚	10
memorial ceremony 名 記念式典	54G
million 形 100万の	10
mind 名 心	22
mix 名 混合	38G
monastery 名 修道院	42G
musical note 名 音符	30G

N

native 形 先住の	54
natural 形 自然な	22
neighborhood 名 地域、近隣住民	38

O

often 副 頻繁に	42
on one's way 副 途中で	50G
organic fertilizer 名 有機肥料	58G
originate 動 発祥する	38G
outlook 名 眺め、展望	58
overall 副 全体的に	18G

P

participate 動 参加する	58
participate in ... 動 …に参加する	18G
partnership 名 提携	14G
perfect 形 申し分のない	46
personal 形 個人的な	54
physical 形 肉体の	22G
pleasant 形 (天気が)気持ちのよい	18
population 名 人口	10
port 名 港	14
portable shrine 名 みこし	38G
predict 動 …を予測する	18
prestigious 形 名声のある	62G

produce 動 …を生産する		62
promote 動 …を促進する		62
public 形 公開の		18
purchase 動 …を購入する		58
put on … 動 …を催す		26G

Q
quality 名 質		22G

R
recently 副 近ごろ		18
recognize 動 …を認識する		42
region 名 地方		62
regularly 副 定期的に		38G
relationship 名 関係		10
repair 動 …を修理する		30
replica 名 レプリカ、複製		30G
representative 名 代表者		54
research 動 …を研究する　名 研究		22
rest 名 残り		14G, 50

S
score 名 楽譜		30G
sculpture 名 彫刻		38
seaweed 名 海藻、海苔		26G
sector 名 部門		14G
seem like 動 …のようである		22
serve 動 (飲食物)を出す		26
settle 動 …に移り住む		54
shelter 形 保護された		54
sightseeing 名 観光		50
similar 形 似ている		14
since 接 …以来、…であるから		18G
site 名 (事件や事業が)行われた場所		66
solid 形 堅実な		54
sort 名 種類		58
souvenir 名 おみやげ		34
state 名 州		26
stone lantern 名 石灯籠		50G
storytelling 名 読み聞かせ		66G
sunny 形 晴れた		18G
support 名 援助		30
surprisingly 副 驚くほど		42G
surround 動 …を囲む		34
surroundings 名 環境		50

T
take place 動 行われる		10G
tea house 名 茶室		14G
technical school 名 専門学校		58G
temple 名 寺		54
theater 名 劇場		42
throughout 副 …の隅から隅まで		34
tie 名 きずな		34
tourism 名 観光事業		62G
trade 名 貿易		14
traditional 形 伝統的な		18
truly 副 本当に		22G

U
unusually 副 非常に		10G

V
valley 名 谷		38
variety 名 多種多様さ		38
vegetable 名 野菜		42
view 名 景色		30
vital 形 きわめて重要な		58

W
waterfront 名 臨海部		46G
wear 動 …を着る		50
weather 名 天気		18G
welcome 動 …を歓迎する		50
well-known 形 よく知られている		10G
wellness 名 健康福祉		22G
while 接 …であるけれども、一方では…		58G
whole 形 全体の		46
widely 副 広く		34
wrap 動 …を包む		26

Y
youth 名 若者		66

クラス用音声 CD 有り（別売）

Twin Cities
—A Cross-cultural Connection
姉妹都市を周遊しながら四技能を身につけよう

2017 年 1 月 20 日　初版発行

著　者　Bradley Gordon Smith / Neil Thomas Millington /
　　　　Anna Millington
発行者　松村達生
発行所　センゲージ ラーニング株式会社
　　　　〒 102-0073　東京都千代田区九段北 1-11-11　第 2 フナトビル 5 階
　　　　電話　03-3511-4392
　　　　FAX　03-3511-4391
　　　　e-mail: elt@cengagejapan.com
　　　　copyright © 2017 センゲージ ラーニング株式会社

装　　丁　森村直美
本文デザイン　有限会社ザイン
組　　版　有限会社ザイン
印刷・製本　株式会社平河工業社

ISBN 978-4-86312-310-6

もし落丁、乱丁、その他不良品がありましたら、お取り替えいたします。
本書の全部または一部を無断で複写（コピー）することは、著作権法上での例外を除き、禁じられていますのでご注意ください。